The Muslim Brotherhood: The History of the Most Influential Islamist Group

By Charles River Editors

Soldiers from the Muslim Brotherhood fighting against Israel in 1948

About Charles River Editors

Charles River Editors provides superior editing and original writing services across the digital publishing industry, with the expertise to create digital content for publishers across a vast range of subject matter. In addition to providing original digital content for third party publishers, we also republish civilization's greatest literary works, bringing them to new generations of readers via ebooks.

Sign up here to receive updates about free books as we publish them, and visit Our Kindle Author Page to browse today's free promotions and our most recently published Kindle titles.

Introduction

Sayyid Qutb

The Muslim Brotherhood

Beginning in 2010, much of the Middle East, including Egypt, was swept up by a series of revolutions later referred to as the Arab Spring. The wave of riots and demonstrations – some violent, some not, but all impactful and sizeable – began in Tunisia before spreading like wildfire to neighboring countries in Northern Africa and eventually into the Arabian Peninsula, including Egypt, Libya, Syria, Yemen, and Bahrain. Though it eventually petered out by mid-2012, the Arab Spring led to the toppling of long-reigning monarchs and regimes, free elections, and attempts to build republics based on democratic principles.

Egypt quickly became one of the most active countries during the Arab Spring, with Tahrir Square in Cairo becoming the focal point of both violent protests and peaceful political demonstrations. Inspired by the protestors in Tunisia, beginning in January 2011, Egyptians rallied to the square and in the streets by the thousands, marching, protesting, and calling for the fall of then-President Hosni Mubarak. Throughout the next several months until the overthrow of Mubarak in February 2011, millions of protesters from a wide range of socio-economic, ethnic, and religious backgrounds demanded a regime change across Egypt.[1]

As significant as it was for the Egyptian people, the Egyptian Arab Spring was a key turning point for the Muslim Brotherhood – Egypt's largest and long-oppressed opposition group. The Brotherhood played a key role in organizing demonstrations, pitting the Egyptian and world media against the Mubarak regime, and orchestrating violent riots and clashes between civilian protestors and the Egyptian security forces, further portraying the regime in a negative light. But it was after the revolution that the Brotherhood truly reaped its rewards; it formed a legal political party and ran in the subsequent parliamentary elections, winning a large number of seats that were previously unavailable to them. Then, in June 2012, the Brotherhood made history in Egypt when it successfully managed to install its candidate Mohamed Morsi as president.[2]

Perhaps no group was surprised by the Egyptian Muslim Brotherhood's swift and largely unopposed rise to power than the Brotherhood itself; for decades, the group had suffered a long history of severe oppression and internal crises, but in the political environment created by the Arab Spring, it only took less than two years for the Brotherhood to control the Egyptian government. As it turned out, it was Islamists who reaped the greatest advantages of the Arab Spring, not only in Egypt, but abroad as well. In Tunisia, the Islamist Nahda party won the largest majority in the post-revolution elections and went on to lead the new government in a country that had endured the dictatorship of President Zine El-Abidine Ben Ali for five decades.[3] Additionally, in other countries across the Arab world, Brotherhood-affiliated or Brotherhood-inspired parties won significant victories that would have been impossible a decade earlier; both the Brotherhood's Justice and Construction Party in Libya and the Muslim Brotherhood in Syria have made definitive gains in establishing political force and influence post-Arab Spring.[4]

As one of the longest surviving yet most controversial political Islamist party in Egypt, the Muslim Brotherhood was long oppressed and forced to operate underground – perhaps more so than in other Arab countries – particularly since the attempted assassination of former Egyptian President Gamal Abdel Nasser by a Muslim Brotherhood member in the early 1950s. The failed attempt triggered a massive crackdown, and for the rest of Nasser's presidency, Brotherhood leaders were rounded up, and its members arrested, tortured, harassed, and exiled.[5] For over six decades since, the Brotherhood tried, failed, then tried again to navigate Egypt's dynamic political environment and maneuver around its semi-authoritarian system, first under nationalist Gamal Abdel Nasser, then under Anwar Sadat, and finally under Hosni Mubarak.

---

[1] "Hosni Mubarak Resigns as President," *Al-Jazeera*, February 11, 2011, http://www.aljazeera.com/news/middleeast/2011/02/201121125158705862.html.
[2] Edmund Blair, "Tables Turn as Egypt's Islamist President Sworn In," *Reuters*, June 30, 2012, http://www.reuters.com/article/2012/06/30/us-egypt-politics-idUSBRE85S0JP20120630.
[3] Richard Spencer, "Tunisia Riots: Reform or Be Overthrown, US Tells Arab States Amid Fresh Riots," *The Telegraph*, January 13, 2011, http://www.telegraph.co.uk/news/worldnews/africaandindianocean/tunisia/8258077/Tunisia-riots-Reform-or-be-overthrown-US-tells-Arab-states-amid-fresh-riots.html.
[4] Alison Pargeter, *The Muslim Brotherhood: From Opposition to Power* (London: Saqi Books, 2013), 6.
[5] Bjorn Olav Utvik, "Filling the vacant throne of Nasser: The economic discourse of Egypt's Islamist Opposition," *Arab Studies Quarterly* 17, no. 4 (Fall 1995), 31.

Despite the gains the group finally made after the Egyptian Arab Spring, as of September 2014, the Brotherhood has reverted to its former position as a banned organization. Mohamed Morsi was toppled by a military coup in July 2013, and on December 25, 2013, the Muslim Brotherhood was officially declared by the Egyptian government a terrorist organization.[6] In the following months, tens of thousands of alleged Brotherhood members and suspected supporters were arrested, tried for vague charges of involvement in violent protests and clashes, and sentenced to jail; in an unprecedented ruling, an Egyptian court went so far as to sentence several hundred to death for their participation in riots that turned violent.[7]

While the Muslim Brotherhood has always been centered in Egypt, its ideology and influence has been exported by many individuals and affiliated groups over the decades, to the extent that just about every radical Sunni group across the Middle East has its roots in the Brotherhood, from Hamas to Osama bin Laden's al-Qaeda. As a result, even as it remained a banned party in Egypt, it retained an outsized influence across the region.

In order to determine the significance of recent events involving the changing political environment in Egypt and the rise and fall of the Muslim Brotherhood, it is necessary to assess the history of the Brotherhood, starting with its beginnings as a loosely knit ideological movement, then exploring its growth into a major political force. *The Muslim Brotherhood* chronicles the history of the group and its widespread influence across the Middle East. Along with pictures of important people, places, and events, you will learn about the Muslim Brotherhood like never before.

---

[6] "Egypt Government Declares Muslim Brotherhood 'Terrorist Group,'" *Ahram Online*, December 26, 2013, http://english.ahram.org.eg/News/90037.aspx.
[7] Helen Williams, "Egypt's Unprecedented Execution Verdicts," *Al-Monitor*, March 24, 2014, http://www.al-monitor.com/pulse/originals/2014/03/egypt-executions.html#.

The Muslim Brotherhood: The History of the Middle East's Most Influential Islamist Group
About Charles River Editors
Introduction
   Chapter 1: The Founding of the Brotherhood
   Chapter 2: Ideology and Organizational Development
   Chapter 3: The Brotherhood in Egypt
   Chapter 4: The Brotherhood under Mubarak
   Chapter 5: The Arab Spring
   Chapter 6: The Brotherhood During and After Morsi
   Chapter 7: The Brotherhood Abroad
   Chapter 8: The Future of the Muslim Brotherhood
   Bibliography

Chapter 1: The Founding of the Brotherhood

In March 1928, a schoolteacher named Hassan al-Banna founded *al-Ikhwan al-Muslimin,* or the Muslim Brotherhood, as an Islamic revivalist movement in the Egyptian town of Ismailia. Though his beginnings were meager, al-Banna was to become one of the most influential 20th century Islamic scholars and ideologues in the region, and the Brotherhood would grow into the world's largest transnational Islamic revivalist organization.

Hassan al-Banna

Hassan al-Banna was born on October 14, 1906 into a poor, pious family in the southern Egyptian town of Mahmudiyya, northwest of Cairo. He was the son of the local imam and mosque teacher, Sheikh Ahmad al-Banna, who was educated at the prestigious al-Azhar University in Cairo and wrote prolifically on Islamic traditions.[8] Hassan's father was an important spiritual influence on Hassan al-Banna, as Sheikh Ahmad ensured that his sons received a pious upbringing that emphasized strong Islamic values.

Though Sheikh Ahmad was of the Hanbali school, which is associated with Sunni Islam,

---

[8] "Hassan Al-Banna and His Political Thought of Islamic Brotherhood," *Ikhwan Web,* May 13, 2008, http://www.ikhwanweb.com/article.php?id=17065.

Hassan himself became engrossed in Sufism, which focuses on more mystical elements of Islam. When he was only twelve years old, Hassan became involved in a Sufi order, and eventually became a fully initiated member in 1922, at the age of sixteen.[9] Hassan's experience with Sufism made a large impact on his conceptualization of the Muslim Brotherhood. As scholar Andrea Mura wrote, "Such [Sufi] influence can be seen in the focus on the spiritual notion of 'brotherhood', as well as on symbolism, rites, the obedience and discipline of adherents (through the traditional oath of loyalty, *bayat*), the title and the strong charismatic tone assumed by al-Banna as the 'Supreme Guide' (*al-murshid al-'amm*), and the spiritual emphasis in al-Banna's message…The notion of Islamic brotherhood is particularly telling because it informs the criteria according to which the 'horizon of the Islamic homeland' is defined. It is the Islamic brotherhood, in the light of its intrinsic 'humanitarianism', that transforms the expansion of Islam into a movement for justice and equality, legitimizing such expansion, and distinguishing it from those forms of conquest and aggression based on mere 'geographic', 'ethnic' or 'racial' factors such as 'nationalism' and 'patriotism.'"[10] Thus, the impact of the softer, more mystical, and more spiritual elements of Sufism played a large role in Hassan building the Brotherhood into more of a socio-religious movement than a hard-line religious organization or a strictly political party.

Hassan al-Banna was only 13 years old when he experienced his first exposure to Egyptian nationalist politics. This was the year of the Egyptian Revolution of 1919, which triggered a series of nationwide protests and revolts against the British occupation of Egypt. Hassan participated in these demonstrations, marking his first brush with not only the opposition movement but Islamic societies and radical youth activists. The revolution eventually led to Britain's recognition of Egyptian independence in 1922.[11]

In 1923, at the age of 14, Hassan entered the Dar al-Ulum in Cairo, a teacher's school that was designed to educate prospective teachers in modern subjects. As it was a less traditional option for education, Hassan's father opposed his son's enrollment, but Hassan proceeded to enroll, marking a break from his conservative Islamic upbringing and his fervent involvement in Sufism. Life in the nation's capital offered Hassan opportunities that he would never have come across had he stayed in his village; he met prominent Islamic scholars, interacted with and joined Islamic societies and youth organizations, and read volumes after volumes of Islamic works. At the same time, Hassan also came across disturbing sights as well; many areas of the city were poverty-ridden, the gap between the wealthy elite and the impoverished was astonishingly great, and the impact of Westernization and secularism could be seen all across the city.[12] According to the Brotherhood's own biography of Hassan, "The four years that Al-Banna spent in Cairo

---

[9] Ibid.
[10] Andrea Mura, "A Genealogical Inquiry into Early Islamism: The Discourse of Hasan Al-Banna," *Journal of Political Ideologies* 17, no. 1 (20120): 72.
[11] "Hassan Al-Banna and His Political Thought of Islamic Brotherhood."
[12] Ibid.

exposed him to the political ferment of the Egyptian capital in the early 1920s, and enhanced his awareness of the extent to which secular and Western ways had penetrated the very fabric of society. It was then that Al-Banna became particularly preoccupied with what he saw as the young generation's drift away from Islam. He believed that the battle for the hearts and minds of the youth would prove critical to the survival of a religion besieged by a Western onslaught. While studying in Cairo, he immersed himself in the writings of the founders of Islamic reformism (the Salafiyya movement), including the Egyptian Muhammad Abduh (1849-1905), under whom his father had studied while at Al-Azhar. But it was Abduh's disciple, the Syrian Rashid Rida (1865-1935), who most influenced Al-Banna."[13]

In 1927, upon graduating from the teacher's school, Hassan was assigned to teach Arabic at a primary school in Ismailia. He threw himself into teaching, not only at the primary school, but through other means as well; he began giving night classes to his students' parents, and also preached in mosques and even coffeehouses.[14] Additionally, while in Ismailia, Hassan witnessed the effects of the British occupation of Egypt, as Ismailia was situated close to the Suez Canal, which was one of the focal points of the British occupation. Hassan increasingly grew disillusioned with the economic, cultural, and military occupation of the British and the negative impact it was having on Egypt and the Egyptian people's adherence to purely Islamic principles and values.

It was for this reason that in March 1928 in Ismailia, Hassan al-Banna established the Muslim Brotherhood, which was back then only one of dozens of other small Islamic associations that were formed in response to the British occupation. The original aim of Hassan was for his newfound organization to provide welfare and charitable services for the population while also educating and Islamizing society.[15] In his first article after the foundation of the Brotherhood, al-Banna criticized not only the Egyptian government but also the Islamic authorities for their quiescence and inability to counter Westernization, secularism, and materialism: "What catastrophe has befallen the souls of the reformers and the spirit of the leaders? What has carried away the ardour of the zealots? What calamity has made them prefer this life to the thereafter? What has made them...consider the way of struggle [*sabil al-jihad*] too rough and difficult?"[16]

In the 1930s, at his own request, Hassan was transferred to a teaching post in Cairo; he likely felt that in order to grow his fledgling organization and make true impact on the current situation in Egypt, he would need to relocate to the capital city. This move to Cairo would eventually be key, as it was here that al-Banna gained thousands of supporters as he continued to preach and garner loyalty and respect, though according to the Muslim Brotherhood's official biography of Hassan al-Banna, "at first, some of [Hassan's] views on relatively minor points of Islamic

---

[13] Ibid.
[14] Ibid.
[15] Mura, ""A Genealogical Inquiry into Early Islamism: The Discourse of Hasan Al-Banna," 69.
[16] Ibid. 70.

practice led to strong disagreements with the local religious elite, and he adopted the policy of avoiding religious controversies."[17] Nonetheless, by the 1940s, the organization was thriving, and it quickly became a potent political and social force in Egypt, attracting significant numbers of not only young students, but also civil servants, professionals, urban laborers, and others who were traditionally less inclined to involve themselves in politics, thus eventually representing almost every group and sector in Egyptian society.

In 1948, when Egypt, Syria, and Jordan went to war with Israel, Hassan was able to send Brotherhood volunteers to fight against the Israelis. However, the 1948 war turned into a miserable and humiliating defeat for the Arab countries, and consequently, the political environment in Egypt turned chaotic as authorities searched for something to blame for the embarrassing defeat and plummeting national morale. Many Brotherhood members began viewing the Egyptian government as betraying the interests of Egyptian nationalism and pride, and in turn, the central authorities began seeing the Muslim Brotherhood as a potential threat to the stability of their power, as well as a possible scapegoat for their failures in war. Though Hassan tried to maintain a tactical alliance with the government, as his organization grew larger, it became impossible for him to maintain full control over every element of his movement. Brotherhood members were subsequently implicated in a number assassinations, most notably that of Prime Minister Mahmoud an-Nukrashi Pasha, who had been convinced that a Brotherhood-led coup plot was brewing and had outlawed the Muslim Brotherhood in December 1948.[18]

As the crackdown on the Islamists continued, the Brotherhood's assets were impounded and its members sent to jail. By the end of January 1949, all contact between Hassan and the government had ceased, and Hassan gave up any hope for a peaceful settlement with the government, instead circulating a small pamphlet clandestinely distributed to Brotherhood members denouncing the order for dissolution issued by the government, and adding that the entire organization could not be held responsible for the actions taken by only several of its members.[19]

The little pamphlet was Hassan's last written work. The final crack of the whip occurred on February 12, 1949 when Hassan al-Banna was shot while walking down a street in Cairo and died a few minutes later in a nearby hospital. Evidence later emerged indicating that the assassination was planned, or at least condoned, by the government, and executed by members of the political police. Those involved in the assassination were only brought to trial after the regime change in 1952.[20]

---

[17] "Hassan Al-Banna and His Political Thought of Islamic Brotherhood."
[18] Joel Gordon, "The False Hopes of 1950: The Wafd's Last Hurrah and the Demise of Egypt's Old Order," *International Journal of Middle East Studies* 21 (1989): 195.
[19] Richard Paul Mitchell, *The Society of the Muslim Brothers* (New York: Oxford University Press, 1993), 69-70.
[20] Ibid., 71.

Chapter 2: Ideology and Organizational Development

At the very least, four different schools of thought or ideologies have come to impact and shape the Brotherhood's own ideology. The first was the reformist movement of the early 1900s that was led by the writings of religious scholars and Islamic revivalists such as Muhammad Abduh. This movement called for society's complete return to pure Islam – or the original sources, including the Qur'an and *hadith* (the teachings and deeds of the Prophet Muhammad) – and rejected any subsequent interpretations of Islamic law made by jurists over the centuries since the Qur'an's writing. The second impact was made by the traditionalist school of thought, which ran in the opposite direction to Abduh's movement, championing heavy reliance on the views and interpretations of jurists and scholars.

The third impactful movement was that sparked by Sayyid Qutb, who was himself a member of the Muslim Brotherhood and today largely known as the father of modern Islamic extremism. The core of Qutbism revolved around a revolutionary and politicized interpretation of the Qur'an, as it divided society into those who belong to Islam or those who oppose it, with almost no grey areas. Qutbism and its impact will be discussed further below. Finally, the fourth movement that impacted the Brotherhood's ideology was that of the Salafist-Wahhabi schools that originated in Saudi Arabia and made its way into Egypt and the Brotherhood in the 1970s. This school of thought centered on a strict and conservative interpretation of the Qur'an and *shari'a*, leaving little room for individual interpretation.[21]

Of these movements, it was perhaps Qutbism that impacted the Brotherhood and its ideology the most, as Sayyid Qutb himself was a prominent and influential member of the Brotherhood. Qutb was born in Egypt in 1906 to a religious family and studied the Qur'an from an early age. Qutb moved to Cairo in 1929 and received a Western education, later becoming a teacher with the government Ministry of Education by the 1930s. His first intellectual pursuits outside of his formal education were in literature, giving him the skills to write novels and literary criticism. In 1939, he became a bureaucrat in the Ministry of Education, where he worked until 1948. Qutb then left Egypt to pursue a master's degree in education in the United States.

While in the United States, he first began thinking and writing about the role of Islam in society. His vision of Islam contrasted sharply with what he perceived to be the immorality of American culture, and the increasing Western influence in his native Egypt as well. Before he had left the United States, he had already published his first major religious work, and he returned to Egypt in 1950.

In 1952, Egypt underwent serious political instability that resulted in a military overthrow of the monarchy. Qutb was heartily pleased with the result, until he realized the military intended to

---

[21] Ibrahim El Houdaiby, *From Prison to Palace: The Muslim Brotherhood's Challenges and Responses in Post-Revolution Egypt* (Fride and Hivos, 2013), 2.

spurn Islamic government for a nationalist one. Qutb began to criticize the new military government, and an attempted assassination of new President Gamal Nasser in 1954 led to a crackdown on the Muslim Brotherhood. By then, Qutb was already an influential member of the Muslim Brotherhood, leading to his imprisonment for the next 10 years.

Qutb after being imprisoned

While in prison, Qutb wrote his two most influential works, *Milestones*, in which Qutb argues for his viewpoint on the political and social role of Islam, and *In the Shade of the Qur'an*, a religious and theological commentary on the Qur'an. Released in 1964, he was rearrested in 1965 and charged with treason. After a trial, he was convicted and executed in 1966.

By the time Qutb had been executed, his work had formed the foundation for the religious studies of the Muslim Brotherhood, and he would become influential for Sunnis throughout the Arab world. After his death, Qutb's brother Muhammad began teaching Islam in Saudi Arabia, where one of his pupils was Ayman al-Zawahiri, who founded the Egyptian Islamic Jihad and mentored Osama bin Laden, with the two of them becoming the leaders of al-Qaeda. Through these connections, Qutb's teachings became influential in al-Qaeda's religious doctrine, as well as other Sunni militant groups like Hamas and Islamic Jihad in the West Bank and Gaza Strip.

Ayman al-Zawahiri

Qutbism does not refer to one fixed ideology, and in fact, is structured on a common foundation of other puritan Islamist schools, such as Wahhabism, Salafism, and Deobandi.[22] As with these other schools, Qutbism is based on the belief that Muslims have deviated from the ways of pure Islam as the Prophet Muhammad had intended, and must return to Islam as it was originally practiced during the time of the Prophet. According to Qutbism, this can only be done through a literal and strict interpretation of the Qur'an and *hadith*, and Muslims should do this not by being slavishly bound to the interpretations made by Islamic scholars, but through their own individual interpretation of the original sources.[23]

Many scholars have argued that the writings of Sayyid Qutb were essential in the formation of not only Islamist movements in Egypt, including the Muslim Brotherhood, but radical Islamist groups abroad. Qutb's goal of a world based only on *shari'a,* his rage against the secular government of Egypt, and his militant interpretation of *jihad* would later inspire Hassan al-Banna and subsequent leaders of the Muslim Brotherhood. In what many call his most important work, *Milestones,* Qutb wrote that God had created Islam for the following purpose: "[Ignorant people] want Islam to become a mere collection of abstractions and theories, the subject of whose application is non-existent conditions. But the course prescribed by God for this religion is the same as it was earlier. First, belief ought to be imprinted on hearts and rule over consciences – that belief which demands that people should not bow before anyone except God or derive laws from any other source. Then, when such a group of people is ready and also against practical

---

[22] Deobandi is a school that is widely represented in the Indian subcontinent and among the South Asian Muslim populations elsewhere across the world. It is a puritan and revivalist movement with Hanafi Sunni Islam, and as with other revivalist movements, condemns the deviation from the original teachings of the Prophet and calls for a return to the pristine ways of Islam.

[23] Dale C. Eikmeier, "Qutbism: An Ideology of Islamic-Fascism," *Parameters* (Spring 2007): 87.

control of society, various laws will be legislated according to the practical needs of that society."[24]

Qutb further went on to write that sharia "is not limited only to legal matters, as some people assign this narrow meaning to the *Sharia*. The fact is that attitudes, the way of living, the values, criteria, habits and traditions, are all legislated and affect people."[25] Qutb also argued that the entire world, including all Muslims, was in a state of *jahiliyah* (ignorance), in which God's true way has completely been replaced by man's corrupt way.

According to Qutb, since *jahiliyah* and Islam cannot coexist, offensive *jihad* was not just allowed but even necessary to destroy the societies based on *jahiliyah* and return the world to Islam.[26] This condoning of offensive *jihad* became a blank check for any Islamic extremist to justify attacks against anyone, Muslim or non-Muslim. As such, after reading the works of Qutb, Islamist groups all over the world began to define this unhindered and complete subjugation to God in all areas of life as the highest form of freedom for all. Even after his death in 1966, Qutb became one of the leading spokesmen of the Brotherhood, rallying the spirits of thousands of hard-line youths and persuasively advocating the use of violence and the waging of violent *jihad* to establish Islamic rule.

Similarly, Hassan al-Banna believed that the revival of pure Islam was the one and only way to cure not only his country, but also the entire Muslim population, of Western domination, inner corruption, and overall civilizational decline. However, Hassan's approach was less revolutionary than that of Qutb; he did not call for *jihad* or the immediate toppling of the current order, but for a more gradualist way. By providing basic service to the community, including building and running schools, hospitals, mosques, and factories, he sought popular support for Islamist goals through pure persuasion. Thus, unlike Qutb, who advocated for a top-down approach that focused on forcibly removing corrupt rulers and governments through *jihad*, Hassan was more bottom-up in his approach, preferring to build an Islamic society by first winning the hearts and minds of the people.

Dr. Johannes J.G. Jansen, a retired Professor of Modern Islamic Thought at the University of Urecht, has written of the rapid expansion of the Brotherhood since its founding in 1928: "A successful new religious movement, like the Mormons, if for clarity's sake I may use that popular appellation, normally expands by a forty percent in ten years. Al-Banna's movement, on the contrary, grew by one hundred percent each year. This incredible but reliably documented percentage means that the Muslim Brotherhood was not your average new religious movement that had to struggle to win over the hearts and minds of the people who crossed its path. The Muslim Brotherhood did not have to convince people of new truths; it was a movement that

---

[24] Sayyid Qutb, "Milestones," in *Political Dissent: A Global Reader: Modern Sources*, ed. Derek Malone-France (Plymouth: Lexington Books, 2012), 229.
[25] James S. Robbins, "Al-Qaeda Versus Democracy," *The Journal of International Security Affairs* 9 (2005): 53-59.
[26] Eikmeier, "Qutbism: An Ideology of Islamic-Fascism," 89.

preached to the converted. Muslims who came into contact with the Brotherhood soon realized that they agreed with the slogans of the Brotherhood, of which the most important are *al-qur'aan dusturnaa wa-l-jihaad sabiiluna*, the Koran is our law and jihad is our way."[27]

Hassan al-Banna therefore gained wide support for his revivalist yet relatively moderate bottom-up approach. His strong stance on the revival and refocus of not just Islam as a religion, but also Islam as a culture and civilization, and his recognition that the people needed to change their mindset just as much as rulers and governments did, led to the organization's rapid growth.

However, Hassan al-Banna's gradualist approach withered after his death, largely because Hassan and his charisma were such key parts of the strategies he espoused. Al-Banna's ideology ultimately eschewed the battleground of theological disputes and political conflicts, avoiding divisive points and emphasizing gradual development. Force was not a large part of his ways, and power even less; though al-Banna's calls for a peaceful and democratic process and gradual change were admirable in an ideal world, he lacked practical tactics and realistic strategies that his successors could inherit and carry on.

After Hassan al-Banna's death, the Brotherhood suffered a widespread crackdown. Sayyid Qutb was one such member of the Brotherhood who was arrested and thrown into prison, and like so many radical thinkers, it was in jail that Qutb's already extreme beliefs were further radicalized; he began to formulate his own extremist ideology for the Brotherhood that built upon al-Banna's existing philosophy. Without their founder, the Brotherhood members turned to Qutb for guidance; he became the chief spokesman in the 1950s and 1960s, and the head of the most powerful sections of the organization, most notably *Qism Nashr al-Da'wah* (the Propagation of the Message Section). In such prominent positions, Qutb was in charge of drafting articles and publishing them, writing and giving speeches and lectures, and the overall spiritual and mental guidance of all Brotherhood members.[28] Finally, he became its martyr in 1966, when he was executed by the Nasser regime.

With the influence of Sayyid Qutb, and building upon what Hassan al-Banna preached, the Muslim Brotherhood's ideology became greatly radicalized. The goal that was once centered on re-teaching Islam to the population developed into a complete reorganization of Muslim society, while shunning non-Muslims and non-orthodox Muslims. Islam was to become the basis for all laws, and it was to be implemented comprehensively instead of in a piecemeal fashion. While the Brotherhood during Hassan al-Banna's time realized the impact of the modernization of the world and of Egypt, and attempted to fit the Brotherhood's ideology into the realities of the world, with Sayyid Qutb's influence, the group began disregarding modern society and its demands.

---

[27] Johannes J.G. Jansen, "The Muslim Brotherhood Movement: A Glance at its History and Ideology," *Gates of Vienna*, http://gatesofvienna.blogspot.jp/2012/07/the-history-and-ideology-of-muslim.html.

[28] Medhini Kumar, "Evaluating The Muslim Brotherhood's Compatibility With Democracy: An Examination of the Ideologies of Hasan Al-Banna, Seyyid Qutb, and Essam El-Erian," (BA diss., Emory College, 2012), 53.

The evolution of the Brotherhood's ideology from that formed by Hassan al-Banna to that of Sayyid Qutb can be characterized by a shift in the group's methods in achieving its goals. While al-Banna was in no way completely innocent of advocating and employing violence, as he had formed a secret apparatus within the Brotherhood that was created for just that purpose, he was significantly more moderate in his thoughts and ways than Qutb, who advocated a violent and offensive *jihad* against all people who he believed threatened his beliefs. Another key difference between the two leaders is that al-Banna was physically there to lead the Brotherhood, whereas Sayyid Qutb spent a majority of his career with the Brotherhood in jail. Qutb developed and wrote down most of his radical ideas in prison, which was secretly distributed to his fellow Brothers, and he never had much opportunity to implement his ideology or explain it in full. It became up to the other members to interpret and implement his writings and beliefs, which led to the emergence of a much more violent interpretation of *jihad* within the Brotherhood.

In the wake of Qutb's death in 1966, the radical Islamists within the Brotherhood who became inspired by Qutb's works regrouped and reorganized the group's structures and ideas. Small militant Islamic groups were formed within the Brotherhood, and the group's educational program was abandoned while plans for a violent overthrow of the ruling regime were explored in depth.[29] Though the group eventually renounced violence in the 1980s and began to channel its resources more toward peaceful political involvement, remnants of its militant ideology remained and continued their activities, particularly during the oppressive reign of Hosni Mubarak.[30]

---

[29] Ibid., 61-62.
[30] Ferry de Kerckhove, *Egypt's Muslim Brotherhood and the Arab Spring* (Calgary: CDFAI, 2012), 1.

Ricardo Stuckert's picture of Mubarak

Chapter 3: The Brotherhood in Egypt

On October 26, 1954, President Gamal Abdel Nasser was shot at eight times as he gave a speech in Cairo to celebrate his securing a full withdrawal treaty with the British. Though Nasser escaped the assassination attempt, it was revealed that the assassin, Mahmoud Abdel Latif, was a Brotherhood member. How much the Brotherhood's leadership knew about the plot, if at all, is unknown, but the government's response was severe. Thousands of Brotherhood members were arrested and imprisoned in the ensuing crackdown, and six men were executed.[31]

---

[31] Pargeter, *The Muslim Brotherhood*, 27.

Nasser

Thus, throughout the 1950s and 1960s, since so many of the membership, including the core leadership, had been imprisoned, the organization crumbled. Though this was Nasser's intention, what he did not expect was for the Brotherhood's resolve to harden even more; the members' spell in prison only hardened and radicalized their beliefs, making them even more determined to challenge the Nasser regime. These hard-line elements were further bolstered by the writings of Qutb and other radical figures in and outside the Brotherhood during a time when the Islamic revivalist movement was sweeping across the Middle East. In a movement that had suffered from a lack of clear direction since the death of its founder and the deterioration of al-Banna's ideology, this radical wind breathed new life into the organization. It was in Qutb that the Brotherhood found a successor to al-Banna as a leader and thinker whose ideas could provide the intellectual justifications for the more militant actions they so craved.

By 1965, the Qutbists within the Brotherhood had formed their own group within the organization, which became known as Organization 1965. It is unclear how much this radical group within the Brotherhood had the support of Hassan al-Hodeibi, who was a close friend to al-Banna and his actual successor, but he was clearly not recognized as the true leader by many of the Brotherhood members, at least not as al-Banna had been. One analyst argued that al-Hodeibi was aware of but did not oppose the emergence of the Qutbists: "Because Qutb's ideological development was not a secret, we can also conclude that al-Hodeibi was aware of the ideological foundation of Organisation 1965. In any case, al-Hodeibi made no effort to object to the group or Qutb's theories, and it can be assumed that he chose to tacitly accept, if not support the activities of Organisation 1965."[32] However, despite his initial hesitation with Organization 1965, once the regime accused it of plotting a regime overthrow and executed a number of those

---

[32] Ibid., 24-27.

allegedly involved, including Sayyid Qutb himself in 1966, al-Hodeibi quickly distanced himself from Organization 1965 to avoid the full disintegration of the Muslim Brotherhood.

Hassan al-Hodeibi

With the death of Qutb and the strengthened crackdown on Brotherhood members and activities, the organization fell into even greater disarray. An internal crisis ensued, with different strands and sects within the Brotherhood unable to compromise and agree on one united mission. Remaining Qutbists and the hard-line elements strongly opposed any conciliatory approach toward the government, and this more radical group eventually split off from the Brotherhood to follow what ultimately was a violent and self-destructive path. On the other hand, al-Hodeibi led the moderates down a more peaceful course as conceived by al-Banna, which could be seen in his published writings during this time, such as *Preachers Not Judges* – largely viewed as an indirect yet pronounced refutation of Qutb's extremist and militant ideas.[33]

On September 28, 1970, Gamal Abdel Nasser died at his residence in Cairo of a heart attack, and Anwar Sadat, as vice president, automatically became acting president.[34] Sadat proved to be a much more lenient president than Nasser; he freed imprisoned Islamists and lifted the ban on the Brotherhood, allowing it to preach and advocate in exchange for its support against his political rivals.[35] The Brotherhood thus began to enjoy the benefits of operating above ground, which they had been prevented from doing since the Egyptian Revolution of 1952 that installed Nasser into power. Under Sadat's rule, the Brotherhood was also able to expand its membership once more into the middle and working classes, and it was even able to recruit members of

---

[33] Ibid., 28.
[34] Craig Diagle, *The Limits of Detente: The United States, the Soviet Union, and the Arab–Israeli Conflict, 1969–1973* (New Haven: Yale University Press, 2012), 115.
[35] Zachary Laub, "Egypt's Muslim Brotherhood," *Council on Foreign Relations*, January 15, 2014, http://www.cfr.org/egypt/egypts-muslim-brotherhood/p23991.

radical student organizations and al-Jama'at al-Islamiyya, another influential Islamist movement in Egypt that had mass popular support, especially among the youth. The Brotherhood and al-Jama'at al-Islamiyya formed an alliance, as a result, cadres of young students with militant aspirations filled the ranks of the Brotherhood. Some of these newcomers were surprised to discover just how meager the Brotherhood's membership was; one student who joined the Brotherhood at this time stated, "When we joined we were shocked to find it was hollow inside. The leaders had cheated us and told us they were the biggest *jama'a* [group]…but when we joined we found it to be empty. In the Al-Minya governorate when we joined we discovered there wasn't a single member of the Ikhwan [Muslim Brotherhood] in it."[36]

Sadat

Anwar Sadat also worked to abolish the one-party system of government that had been

---

[36] Pargeter, *The Muslim Brotherhood*, 33.

installed by his predecessor. Prior to the 1970s, the Arab Socialist Union established by Nasser had been the sole party in government, but under Sadat, the Brotherhood was able to mobilize politically and freely. This triggered a new period in the history of the organization, as the possibility of actually obtaining real political power became a reality.[37] The Brotherhood's militant aspirations gradually disappeared, and instead, the group began outlining political goals and objectives.

Despite the freedom that the group enjoyed under Sadat, the Brotherhood still faced challenges. Sadat had aspirations of a peaceful reconciliation with Israel, and to achieve this, he became a stalwart ally of the United States and befriended Western leaders. On November 19, 1977, Anwar Sadat surprised the world with his dramatic arrival in Jerusalem, becoming the first Arab leader to visit Israeli soil and deliver a speech to the Knesset.[38] In September 1978, with the hope to finally settle a peace treaty once and for all, President Jimmy Carter invited Anwar Sadat and Israeli Prime Minister Menachem Begin to Camp David in Washington D.C. For eleven days, the three leaders negotiated, discussed, and argued. On September 17, 1978, the two sides were finally able to agree on a framework for peace. In short, the framework stipulated that Israel will execute a full withdrawal from the Sinai Peninsula over a three-year period, while Egypt would develop full peaceful relations with Israel. The fact that there should be transitional agreements established for the West Bank and Gaza, and for continued discussion over the status of Palestinians and Jewish settlers in the occupied territories, was also included.[39]

Sadat's alliance with the West and his aspirations for peace with Israel were problematic for the Muslim Brotherhood, as Sadat's position conflicted with the goals and views of the Brotherhood. The organization was initially immovable in their opinion against Sadat's foreign policy, though later their position eased. More importantly, the Brotherhood's anti-Israel stance represented the voice of some Egyptians, who were still raw from their defeat in the 1967 war against Israel.

Thus, Sadat's reign heralded great changes in Egypt, leading to positive reform such as the liberalization and democratization of the Egyptian political arena. However, this also led to his aligning with the West on many occasions; therefore, despite his significantly more lenient stance toward the Brotherhood, his support of the Western powers and cooperation with Israel placed him in a compromising position with the Brotherhood and other hard-line Islamists. This forced the Brotherhood to reassess its constituency and reconsider its relationship with the Sadat government, as the Brotherhood could not budge on its position against Israel, nor could it fully embrace such high levels of relations with the West. The Brotherhood began utilizing the flexibility given to them to launch criticisms of Sadat by publishing critical articles and

---

[37] Saad Eddin Ibrahim. *Egypt, Islam, and Democracy: Twelve Critical Essays* (Cairo: American University of Cairo Press, 1996), 37.
[38] Elbendary, "The Long Revolution."
[39] "The Camp David Accords of 1979," *BBC News*, November 29, 2001, http://news.bbc.co.uk/2/hi/in_depth/middle_east/israel_and_the_palestinians/key_documents/1632849.stm.

organizing anti-government demonstrations.

In 1979, the Iranian Revolution swept across the Middle East – the first revolution of its kind to be fueled by a political and radicalized form of Islam. The resulting short-term and long-term effects of the revolution were significant; Islamic fundamentalist and revivalist movements, inspired by the success of the Iranian clerics, began forming and plotting their own revolution in their respective countries – including in Egypt. The Islamist experience in Iran had proven that an Islamic state was possible, and the Brotherhood grew motivated to branch away from the ways of its predecessors, who had relied on discussions of ideology and Islamic theories, and instead go down a more realistic path, focusing on practical socio-economic challenges in Egypt, like poverty and government corruption. Criticisms against the Sadat regime, fueled by the Brotherhood, increased and spread across the country. Brotherhood leaders began entering seemingly secular organizations to consolidate their influence, such as activist groups and professional syndicates and unions, and members reached out to the people by offering welfare services like education and health care, filling the gaps where the state was inadequate.[40]

Chapter 4: The Brotherhood under Mubarak

On October 6, 1981, Anwar Sadat was assassinated during a victory parade honoring the eight anniversary of the Egyptian victory in the 1973 Yom Kippur War. A radical militant Islamist group, the Egyptian Islamic Jihad, claimed responsibility.[41] Sadat's fall led to the rise of his vice president, Hosni Mubarak, who would go on to rule Egypt for three long decades.

Hosni Mubarak immediately began a major clampdown on the Muslim Brotherhood, resulting in a number of leaders and key figures, most of them the more militant and hard-line members within the Brotherhood, becoming imprisoned or exiled. This removal of the more extremist elements of the Brotherhood led to the moderate reformists within the group seizing control and leading the group down the path of political participation. As one member of the Brotherhood recalled, "By the 1980s, the demand for *shari'a* had receded and was replaced by calls for freedom to establish political parties and join elections and have newspapers."[42]

Since the ouster of radical elements from the Brotherhood, the Mubarak regime grew tolerant of the group, but nonetheless, it still imposed restrictions on its activities, and officially, the group remained a banned organization. Despite being outlawed, the Brotherhood was able to take advantage of the political and social liberalization of Egypt in the 1980s by increasing its membership and engaging in politics. Because it still remained an illegal organization, the Brotherhood participated in parliamentary elections by joining the list of recognized political parties; in 1984, Brotherhood candidates ran as part of the Wafd party, and the Muslim Brotherhood-Wafd alliance was able to obtain 15% of the vote, or 58 seats, of which 8 were won

---

[40] Pargeter, *The Muslim Brotherhood*, 34.
[41] "Anwar Sadat Killed," *UPI*, 1981, http://www.upi.com/Archives/Audio/Events-of-1981/Anwar-Sadat-Killed.
[42] Pargeter, *The Muslim Brotherhood*, 35.

by Brotherhood candidates. Again in 1987, the Brotherhood formed an alliance with the Labor and Liberal parties, and the alliance won 17% of the vote, or 56 seats, of which 36 were occupied by Brotherhood members.[43] Additionally, the Brotherhood continued to expand its membership and place its members in key professional associations and syndicates, in including the influential Doctors Syndicate.

However, despite the Brotherhood's transition from militant activities to political participation, marking its shift to a more non-confrontational approach, the 1990s saw the re-oppression of the Brotherhood when the group's vocal position against Egypt's participation in the Second Gulf War clashed with the government's support of the U.S.-led military intervention in Kuwait. Additionally, in October 1992, when the Dashour Earthquake occurred in southern Egypt, the Brotherhood was able to show its capacity for serving the Egyptian people far more than the government was able to by organizing relief efforts and creating shelters, health clinics, schools, and providing food and clothing for the victims.[44] Through demonstrations and community service programs, the Brotherhood enjoyed a rapid expansion of its network across Egypt.

The government again returned to repressive measures to stem the Brotherhood's burgeoning popularity and influence. Brotherhood offices were raided, members and supporters were rounded up, and Brotherhood candidates were prevented from participating in parliamentary elections. In 1993, a law was passed that dismantled the boards of the many influential professional unions and syndicates that the Brotherhood controlled and put them under a government-appointed administrative board.[45]

The government repression resulted in another round of inner conflict within the Brotherhood, as hardened older members who dominated the leadership clashed with the middle generation of younger leaders, who favored conciliatory measures – namely, increased cooperation with other political trends, a more focused effort to gain legality and legitimacy as a political and liberal party, as well as greater openness within the organization so that members can more openly debate on the future of the Brotherhood. In 1998, a group of prominent middle generation leaders decided to leave the Brotherhood and form a new political party called Wasat, with the intention to lead an Islamic yet more pluralistic approach to achieve change in Egypt.[46]

After several years of reorganization and reevaluation, the Brotherhood began making a comeback in 2000, when Brotherhood members ran as independents and won 17 seats.[47] The Brotherhood also altered its previous Qutbist position against non-Muslims and began openly

---

[43] "Politics and the Brotherhood in the Mubarak Era," *Islamopedia*, http://www.islamopediaonline.org/country-profile/egypt/politics-and-muslim-brotherhood/politics-and-brotherhood-mubarak-era.
[44] Ibid.
[45] Ibid.
[46] Augustus R. Norton, *Thwarted Politics: The Case of Hizb al-Wasat. Remaking Muslim Politics: Pluralism, Contestation, Democratization*, R.W. Hefner, ed. Princeton: Princeton University Press, 2005, 133.
[47] International Crisis Group (ICG). 20 April 2004. "Islamism in North Africa II: Egypt's Opportunity". Cairo/Brussels: International Crisis Group., 12.

accepting the participation of Copts and other religious minorities, which the group justified by pointing out that Hassan al-Banna himself had two Copts as his assistants.[48] Also in public statements, the Brotherhood worked to shed its image of religious intolerance by denouncing the anti-Semitism it had expressed in its publications in the past several decades. Mohammad Mahdi Akef, who was elected the Brotherhood's Supreme Guide in 2004, stated in an interview with Al-Jazeera, "We follow our religion and Prophet in dealing with all people in a respectful way. Islam dignifies Christians and Jews and we hope they treat us the same way. The ignorance of people is what is causing a grudge among them and not their religion."[49] Such a statement would have never been heard out of the mouths of Brotherhood members during the 1960s and 1970s.

In the following years under Mubarak's rule, the Brotherhood continued to work to participate in politics while also maintaining an ongoing internal debate about what exactly the Brotherhood stood for and what exactly its goals were. In the 2005 parliamentary elections, the organization won an astonishing 88 seats, seizing control of 20% of the parliamentary seats, despite the government's arrest of hundreds of its supporters.[50] This cycle of the Brotherhood attempting to gain more political influence and the government responding with a new wave of crackdowns continued until the end of 2010, when popular protests broke out in Tunisia and spread to the rest of the Middle East. The Brotherhood was shaken out of its inertia and forced to look beyond its internal crises and ambiguous strategies to decide what role it would play in the Arab Spring and the new Egypt that emerged out of it.

Chapter 5: The Arab Spring

On December 17, 2010, a 26 year old Tunisian fruit vendor named Mohamed Bouazizi set himself on fire in an act of protest against the confiscation of his goods and the humiliation he received after attempting to retrieve his wares from government officials. His act represented the frustrations of thousands of Tunisians and Arabs alike, who were all tired of the rampant corruption in their governments and the poverty in their streets. The fury that spread across Tunisia quickly turned into an outright revolution, and the event also became a catalyst for the wider Arab Spring as Bouazizi's act of self-immolation sparked an explosion of demonstrations and violent protests in several other Arab and non-Arab countries. Several weeks later, on January 14, 2011, Tunisian President Zine El Abidine Ben Ali announced his abdication, putting an end to his 23 years in power.[51]

That one man had triggered the downfall of a long-reigning autocracy showed that change was

---

[48] Ibid., 14.
[49] Doha Al-Zohairy, "Muslim Brotherhood: We Are a Power in Egypt," *Al-Jazeera,* June 22, 2005, http://web.archive.org/web/20060427063406/http://english.aljazeera.net/NR/exeres/52642A0D-2FC0-4616-8308-19972B99E70F.htm.
[50] International Republican Institute, December 2005, "2005 Parliamentary Election Assessment in Egypt," International Republican Institute Report, 15.
[51] Robert F. Worth, "How a Single Match Can Ignite a Revolution," *The New York Times,* January 21, 2011, http://www.nytimes.com/2011/01/23/weekinreview/23worth.html?src=twrhp&_r=0.

possible, and the swiftness and relative ease with which the Tunisian Revolution succeeded further inspired other disgruntled Muslim populations across the world. In Egypt, the events in Tunisia prompted thousands of young Egyptians to take to the streets, calling for Mubarak's resignation. Protests began on January 25, 2011, with a large bulk of the demonstrators gathering in Cairo's Tahrir Square, which eventually became the central site for protests. Though Mubarak attempted to fight the demonstrations by sending in security forces and limiting the country's Internet access to stymie the protestors' ability to organize through social media communications, by February of 2011, it was clear to Mubarak, Egypt, and the world that the revolution in Egypt was irreversible. On February 10, 2011, Mubarak resigned and ceded all presidential power to Vice President Omar Suleiman.[52]

Suleiman

---

[52] Chris McGreal and Jack Shenker, "Hosni Mubarak Resigns – and Egypt Celebrates a New Dawn," *The Guardian*, February 11, 2011, http://www.theguardian.com/world/2011/feb/11/hosni-mubarak-resigns-egypt-cairo.

When protests in Egypt first began on January 25, 2011 – or the Day of Rage, as it came to be known – the Muslim Brotherhood was just as surprised as Mubarak at the ferocity of the people's sudden show of frustrations. This was because it was not the Islamists who first stood up in protest and risked their lives to bring the revolution to Egypt but the secular youth. Thus, despite being one of the largest, oldest, and most established opposition groups in Egypt, the Muslim Brotherhood had no role in the initial outbreak of demonstrations, and in fact, was completely outmaneuvered by the younger generation that did not hold up the Qur'an or shout for a return to Islam as they protested but instead held smartphones and tweeted their demands.

Of course, this did not mean that the Muslim Brotherhood was completely unaware of the events in Tunisia, or that it did not anticipate that this could be a chance for it to bring change to Egypt. Just days after Tunisian President Zine El Abidine Ben Ali fled Tunis, Mohamed Morsi, who was then a leading Guidance Bureau member within the Brotherhood, issued a statement to the Mubarak regime laying out several key demands: the immediate dissolution of parliament and the holding of free and fair elections; the amending of the constitution; free and fair presidential elections; and the formation of a new government of national unity. Morsi also warned of vague repercussions if the Mubarak regime failed to respond to the demands, but he stopped short of actually demanding that Mubarak step aside. The threat was weak and indirect, and the Brotherhood clearly failed to understand that this was not a time for words and statements but action.[53]

---

[53] Pargeter, *The Muslim Brotherhood*, 163.

Wilson Dias' picture of Morsi

Where the Brotherhood failed to act, secular youths and student activists filled in, organizing the Day of Rage. Participating in the protests was deemed risky for the Brotherhood, as the group was reluctant to get involved in something that may or may not bring down the regime; the uncertainty made it difficult for the Brotherhood to participate, as it did not want to risk taking any actions that might later be deemed traitorous, forcing it to lose all the gains it had made over the past decades. Though individual Brotherhood members likely participated in the protests, the organization itself did not issue an official call for its members to participate, nor did it list itself among the organizers of the protests. Moreover, ever since the group renounced violence in the 1980s, the group had shied away from the label of a revolutionary movement, instead focusing on working within the established order than working to overthrow it. That one of the nation's most powerful opposition groups did not give its official support to the demonstrations was seen as contradictory to many, but the Brotherhood's fear of becoming the scapegoat once more overpowered its aspirations for a new Egypt.[54]

However, as several days of protests followed the Day of Rage and it became more and more apparent that this was not a temporary spark of frustration, the Brotherhood realized that the tides were turning and it could not stand back any longer. If the people were going to overthrow the Mubarak regime, as the people had done in Tunisia, the Brotherhood could not afford to lose the opportunity to lead the nation-building that would surely follow. As such, by January 28, 2011, the Brotherhood fully and officially endorsed the protests and joined the demonstrations. Yet, despite the Brotherhood's endorsement, it was still reluctant to take a significant leadership role in the revolution. As Mohamed Morsi put it, "We are not pushing this movement, but we are moving with it. We don't wish to lead it but we want to be part of it." [55]

There was another pragmatic element to the Brotherhood's hesitation to take a prominent role in the revolution. As mentioned earlier, the organization had been blamed countless times in the past and disgraced as a violent, extremist, and radical organization. Knowing this, the Brotherhood did not wish to provide the regime with any more ammunition to reject or delegitimize the revolution. As prominent Muslim Brotherhood member and Deputy to the Supreme Guide Rashad al-Bayoumi explained, "We are keeping a low profile as an organization. We are not marching with our slogans. We don't want this revolution to be portrayed as a revolution of the Muslim Brothers, as an Islamic revolution."[56] This pragmatic and rational mindset that the Brotherhood displayed showed maturity and growth on the part of the group; it was well aware, after decades of experience, that if it took a leading role in the revolution, Mubarak, his allies, and much of the world would quickly denounce it as a bid by radical Islamists to seize power. Not just in Egypt, but in much of the Middle East, Islamists had long been portrayed as power-hungry extremists and great threats to Western and global interests.

Though it therefore kept a fairly low profile, the Brotherhood did play a key and leading role in the protests, albeit quietly and from the shadows. Drawing on years of experience in grassroots activities and using its vast networks and resources built throughout its decades of social and welfare programs, Brotherhood members set up tents in Tahrir Square, distributed food and hot tea for the demonstrators, donated blankets and warm clothing, and set up an emergency first aid clinic. The Brotherhood also printed and posted fliers and banners, set up audio equipment in Tahrir Square for speeches to be heard, and regulated entry and exit points to the square to prevent government-hired disturbers from gaining entry. As one young Brotherhood member declared, "We are the best in Egypt to organize."[57] Still, as much as the Brotherhood was

---

[54] Ibid., 163-164.
[55] Peter Beaumont and Jack Shenker, "Egypt Braces Itself for Biggest Day of Protests Yet," *The Guardian*, January 27, 2011, http://www.theguardian.com/world/2011/jan/27/egypt-protests-biggest-day-yet.
[56] "Muslim Brotherhood's Rashad al-Bayoumi: 'The Revolution Will Continue Until Our Demands Are Met'," *Spiegel Online International*, February 7, 2011, http://www.spiegel.de/international/world/muslim-brotherhood-s-rashad-al-bayoumi-the-revolution-will-continue-until-our-demands-are-met-a-743919.html.
[57] Pargeter, *The Muslim Brotherhood*, 165-166.

involved in the behind-the-scenes activities of the revolution, it remained reluctant to lead the protests, take on interviews, or make speeches.

This changed in early February, however, when it became even clearer that the end was near for the Mubarak regime. Finally sensing its opportunity, the Brotherhood intensified its involvement in the revolution by officially demanding the resignation of Mubarak, directly placing itself in the Mubarak regime's line of fire. It began identifying itself as the representatives of the people, placing itself in the forefront of the opposition, and it was at this time that some members of the Brotherhood began openly demonstrating with copies of the Qur'an in Tahrir Square. The sudden emergence of the Brotherhood from the shadows of the revolution did elicit some response from secular protestors, who criticized the group for hijacking the revolution, and this forced Brotherhood members to assure the people that it had no private agendas, nor was it planning to take senior posts in the post-Mubarak government. On February 4, 2011, senior Brotherhood member Mohammed al-Beltagi released a statement assuring Egyptians that the Brotherhood was "ready to negotiate after [the end of] the Mubarak regime," and that Brotherhood leaders have "said clearly that we have no ambitions to run for the presidency, or posts in a coalition government."[58]

As Mubarak announced he was stepping down, political parties, including the Brotherhood, entered into dialogue with Vice President Omar Suleiman. The Brotherhood continued to take a cautious approach, reasserting that it was not interested in seizing power. Several days after Mubarak's departure, senior Brotherhood member Essam el-Erian stated to the Associated Press that the Brotherhood was not running any candidates for the upcoming presidential elections, as such a move would be "too controversial," and he added that "we are also not targeting to have a majority in the upcoming parliament. This is a time for solidarity, unity, we need a national consensus."[59] While reassuring the post-Mubarak military regime that the Brotherhood had no intention of challenging the military, the organization also made sure it maintained a presence in Tahrir Square, where protestors continued to demonstrate, demanding the military hand over power to a civilian government. The Brotherhood therefore fell back to its age-old strategy of maneuvering between different camps and forging temporary alliances of convenience so that it had positive ties with both sides: the new military regime and the protesting populace.

In April 2011, the Brotherhood established a political party called the Freedom and Justice Party (FJP), with Mohamed Morsi appointed as party head. On May 18, 2011, the Brotherhood formally submitted a request to form the party, which reportedly had some 9,000 members.[60] Though the Brotherhood and FJP both claimed that the two organizations were completely separate entities, this could not be farther from the truth, as party leaders were appointed by the

---

[58] Tom Perry, "Brotherhood Says No Plans for Egypt Presidential Bid," *Reuters*, February 4, 2011, http://af.reuters.com/article/egyptNews/idAFLDE71309L20110204.
[59] "Egypt: Muslim Brotherhood Plans Political Party," *USA Today*, February 15, 2011, http://usatoday30.usatoday.com/news/world/2011-02-15-egypt-muslim-brotherhood_N.htm.
[60] Pargeter, *The Muslim Brotherhood*, 173.

Brotherhood's Guidance Bureau, the Brotherhood wrote the FJP's party platform, and Brotherhood members were prohibited from joining any party other than the FJP.[61] Furthermore, as the elections neared, the Brotherhood became more and more confident that it would win a significant number of seats, despite its initial announcement that it would not run in the elections. After decades of clandestine activities and underground opposition, power was finally within the Brotherhood's reach, and it was not going to miss this opportunity.

In the parliamentary elections, which lasted from November 2011 to January 2012, the FJP and its coalition took 235 seats, or 47.2%, making it the largest bloc in parliament.[62] Furthermore, in the presidential elections, the Brotherhood candidate, Mohamed Morsi, won with 51.73% of the vote.[63] On June 24, 2011, Morsi was declared the president of post-Mubarak Egypt, and the Muslim Brotherhood's sudden transformation from an illegal and furtive movement to the ruling power was complete.

It is interesting to note the paradoxical nature of the Brotherhood's ascendancy to power. The Brotherhood, throughout its history, has always been a movement that had shunned coups and revolutions, declaring itself to be uninterested in seizing power. Even while the revolution was unfolding, and even when all signs pointed to Mubarak's resignation, the Brotherhood still continued to insist that it had no interest in ruling. Instead, it proclaimed itself a group of the people, purportedly preferring to work from the bottom up and educating society on Islam and Islamic rule in order to prepare it to the eventual establishment of an Islamic state.[64] However, when the opportunity arose and power was within its reach, the Brotherhood rushed at the chance to grab it and rule. The group was able to mobilize its forces and resources at such an unprecedented level, and influence the protesters so skillfully, that it was able to maneuver its way through the transition process and dominate the emergent new government.

That said, many scholars would argue that this seeming paradox was not at all surprising, and in fact, it should have been expected of such a historically controversial organization. The group has long battled against its contradictions, which has made it difficult to pin itself down to one dominant platform and work to amass unwavering popular support. Furthermore, the structure of the Brotherhood is also complex: it is a social movement that also functions as a political entity; it is a transnational organization that has branches in countries across Northern Africa and the Middle East; it has proclaimed to be non-violent yet organizes and participates in violent rallies and protests; and it has long denounced the West but also works with Western media to be seen as a moderate organization that upholds progressive, democratic, and inclusive values and policies.

---

[61] Ibid., 174.
[62] Ibid., 177.
[63] Ibid., 181.
[64] Pargeter, *The Muslim Brotherhood*, 7.

Chapter 6: The Brotherhood During and After Morsi

In a short period of time, the Brotherhood had risen to the top with little opposition, but perhaps because the group had not initially expected to attain such great power so quickly, the Brotherhood struggled in its new leadership role. As president, Mohamed Morsi granted himself sweeping powers, including unlimited powers to pass legislations without judicial oversight. Additionally, the Brotherhood continued to install its members into key government and parliamentary posts, almost as if it had completely erased its memory of its previous reluctance to play a significant role in the post-revolution government. As author Yasmine El Rashidi wrote, "In the press you could read that the Brotherhood was engaged in one "power grab" after another – of the parliament, the cabinet, the press itself…and another power grab during the drafting of the constitution of the new, democratic Egypt. What was meant to be a 'representative' one-hundred-member Constitutional Assembly had been turned, by the Islamist-led parliament, into an Islamist-dominated one, and one in which the Islamists – the Muslim Brotherhood members but also ultra-orthodox Salafis – were trying, increasingly, to impose their own rigid, radical views."[65]

In fact, Morsi gave himself more powers than even Mubarak had during his long-running autocracy. In late November 2012, he issued a draft constitution and called for a national referendum, which his opponents called an "Islamist coup," though Morsi assured the nation that his actions were only to secure a "democratic transition." Many of Morsi's advisors resigned in protest against his unprecedented consolidation of power, and newspapers wrote that the "true colors" of the Brotherhood had been revealed with "Morsi's power grab."[66] By December 2012, thousands of protestors filled Tahrir Square and marched down the streets of Cairo, calling for an end to the dictatorship that they had so fiercely fought to bury during the Egyptian Arab Spring.

---

[65] Yasmine El Rashidi, "Egypt: The Rule of the Brotherhood," *The New York Review of Books*, February 7, 2013, http://www.nybooks.com/articles/archives/2013/feb/07/egypt-rule-brotherhood/?pagination=false.
[66] Ibid.

Lilian Wagdy's photo of an anti-Morsi protest in 2013

On July 3, 2013, the Egyptian armed forces made their move. Mohamed Morsi was arrested by senior members of the military and placed under house arrest, while dozens of his top supporters and Muslim Brotherhood leaders were rounded up. The coup prompted cheers from the opposition and outrage from the Islamists. General Abdel Fattah El-Sisi, Egypt's top military officer who later became president in June 2014, announced that the military was merely "fulfilling its historic responsibility to protect the country."[67] In the months that followed, Morsi and many of the top Muslim Brotherhood figures were placed on trial. The Muslim Brotherhood was officially declared a terrorist organization on December 25, 2013, and members and supporters continue to be arrested, sentenced, and imprisoned.

---

[67] Ben Wedeman, Reza Sayah, and Matt Smith, "Coup Topples Egypt's Morsy; Deposed President under 'House Arrest,'" *CNN*, July 4, 2013, http://edition.cnn.com/2013/07/03/world/meast/egypt-protests/index.html?hpt=hp_t1.

A photo of the dispersal of pro-Morsi protesters in August 2013

Sisi

A poll on the Muslim Brotherhood's official English website asks: "After the military coup against democracy in Egypt, should the Muslim Brotherhood participate in future elections?" The choice is limited to a simple "yes" or "no," and as of September 6, 2014, the site showed that a total of 8,480 visitors had voted, with 63.7% voting "yes," and 36.3% voting "no."[68] The Brotherhood has therefore been thrown back to its original state as an illegal organization that is internally battling between its hard-line elements and its moderate voices. It appears that despite its fight for power, and despite finally achieving it, the Muslim Brotherhood was woefully unprepared to rule.

Chapter 7: The Brotherhood Abroad

Since its creation in 1928, the Muslim Brotherhood has grown not only within Egypt but internationally as well. Although the Egyptian branch undoubtedly remains the most influential Brotherhood group, in the past few decades, the Brotherhood brand and its ideology have reached global status, to the extent that it wields influence in almost every state with a Muslim population. Today, there are branches and affiliated parties in Jordan, Syria, Bahrain, Tunisia, Algeria, Iraq, Sudan, Somalia, Yemen, as well as the presence of Hamas in the Gaza Strip, West Bank, Qatar, and Turkey. That said, exactly how much these branches coordinate with each

---

[68] "Ikhwan Web," accessed September 6, 2014, http://www.ikhwanweb.com/.

other, or whether they have any significant relations at all, remains unclear. The greatest factor in this is that each country is different in its governance structure, relationship between state and religion, and societal characteristics, so the ideological affiliations that link these various Brotherhood branches are subject to the national environments that shape each individually.

The diffusion of the Brotherhood ideology across the Middle East began decades ago when the Egyptian Muslim Brotherhood was suppressed by Gamal Abdel Nasser in the 1960s and its members exiled across Europe and the Arab world. In the early 1980s, the Egyptian Brotherhood sought to establish some degree of coordination among the various branches scattered across the world, but understandably, that proved difficult; as prominent leader of the Sudanese Muslim Brotherhood Hasan al-Turabi noted: "You cannot run the world from Cairo."[69]

Making matters more complicated, as Brotherhood branches flourished in various Arab countries, each branch began forming and developing its own goals and political stances. For example, the Brotherhood branches in Egypt and Jordan have historically been critical of the United States, though both have on occasion considered alliances and partnerships with the U.S. when the branches deemed it advantageous. On the contrary, the Syrian Brotherhood during the Bush Administration openly supported Washington's efforts to pressure and isolate the regime of President Bashar Assad, and thus, the inflammatory anti-U.S. statements heard in Cairo and Amman were rare in Damascus. Even when it comes to Israel – inarguably one of the most important issues for the Brotherhood – there is no united stance among the various branches. Egyptian Muslim Brotherhood members have made public anti-Semitic statements in the past, including Yusuf al-Qardawi, an exiled Egyptian Brotherhood leader. Al-Qardawi has been banned from and denied reentry into the U.S., U.K., and Ireland for his controversial and extremist statements against Israel and Western countries.[70] In contrast, Kamal El Helbawi, who is reportedly the most influential Brotherhood member in the U.K., has been lauded for his speeches calling for neighborliness and better Arab-Israeli relations.[71]

Thus, it appears the various branches of the Brotherhood have and will for the foreseeable future remain divided in their views and goals. It is therefore prudent to analyze each Brotherhood branch on its own and within its own environment instead of searching for links. Though the basic Islamist ideology may be similar, if not the same, each branch operates in unique political, economic, and social circumstances that in turn shape the mission of the branch.

The Brotherhood in the Levant

---

[69] Robert S. Leiken and Steven Brooke, "The Moderate Muslim Brotherhood," *Foreign Affairs*, 2007, http://www.foreignaffairs.com/articles/62453/robert-s-leiken-and-steven-brooke/the-moderate-muslim-brotherhood.
[70] Shane Phelan, "'Fatwa' Sheikh with Links to Irish Muslims Is Refused Visa," *Independent.ie*, August 8, 2011, http://www.independent.ie/irish-news/fatwa-sheikh-with-links-to-irish-muslims-is-refused-visa-26759225.html.
[71] Leiken and Brooke, "The Moderate Muslim Brotherhood."

The Jordanian Brotherhood was formed in 1945, and unlike many of the other branches, it is a recognized legal political and social party in Jordan. Though the Jordanian branch follows the Islamist agenda of the Egyptian branch, the Jordanian Brotherhood is exceedingly more moderate and has always rejected any use of violence. Despite Amman's violent history of brutally suppressing opposition parties, especially Islamist ones, the Jordanian Brotherhood was able to survive largely because it has always ensured that it played within the boundaries and the rules established by the government.

Thus, the branch in Jordan is passive yet still very much active. Since the 1950s, it has worked to build schools, hospitals, youth clubs, and charities, and dabbled in the political scene to the extent allowed by the regime. Its political wing, the Islamic Action Front (IAF), was founded in 1992, and has since participated actively in Jordanian politics, winning an adequate number of seats each election.[72] The IAF is decidedly more liberal than Islamist parties in other countries, as it espouses democracy, pluralism, religious tolerance, and women's rights as key to Jordan's development as a modern nation and key player in Middle Eastern politics. Though Brotherhood branches in other Arab countries have been, and continued to be, oppressed to some degree, particularly since the Arab Spring, the IAF and Jordanian Brotherhood continue to enjoy rights and freedoms that no other Brotherhood branch has ever enjoyed.

At the other end of the spectrum lies the Syrian Muslim Brotherhood. Of all the Muslim Brotherhood branches scattered across the world, the Syrian one likely has the most eventful and controversial history, as it has operated in a country and under a regime that was brutally oppressive and violently autocratic. The group experienced severe crackdowns, debilitating internal disputes and divisions, and forced exile, making it remarkable that the Syrian Brotherhood has been able to survive at all.

The Syrian Muslim Brotherhood was officially founded on February 3, 1945, when it registered with the Syrian Interior Ministry and released its manifesto. The Syrian Brotherhood at the time of its founding had links with the Egyptian branch; in fact, Hassan al-Banna himself supervised its creation. In spite of this, there were notable differences between the two branches; the Syrian branch was more open to the idea of pan-Arabism whereas the Egyptian Brotherhood focused solely on Egyptian politics. The Syrian branch was also more welcoming of other minorities and ideological groups, reflecting the general political moderation that occurred in 1950s Syria between the leftwing Communist-Ba'athists and the rightwing camp supporting the West and Iraq.[73] The Syrian Brotherhood has since worked to portray itself as a moderate Islamist group, and the group's strategy continues today; in April 2012, the group unveiled a manifesto that "did not mention the word Islam and continued pledges to respect individual

---

[72] Syed Saleem Shahzad, "Jordan's Islamic Front Rallies Muslims," *Asia Times*, March 7, 2003, http://www.atimes.com/atimes/Middle_East/EC07Ak01.html.

[73] Mohammad Saied Rassas, "Syria's Muslim Brotherhood: Past and Present," *Al-Monitor*, January 5, 2014, http://www.al-monitor.com/pulse/politics/2014/01/syria-muslim-brotherhood-past-present.html#.

rights."[74]

Despite its allegedly moderate views, the Brotherhood experienced severe repression in Syria. This was regardless of the fact that the Syrian Brotherhood was founded by scholars with ties to powerful Sunni elites and landowners of major cities like Aleppo and Hama, in contrast to the Egyptian Brotherhood, which had been founded by a schoolteacher with no ties to the political elite. In 1958, Egypt and Syria formed a political union called the United Arab Republic, but the Syrian Muslim Brotherhood was swiftly banned, as it had been in Egypt under Nasser. The Brotherhood subsequently participated in the dissent against the ruling secularist Ba'ath Party during the 1970s and early 1980s, as membership in the Syrian Brotherhood became a capital offense in 1980.[75] Following the violent Hama uprising of 1982, which led to the massacre of thousands of civilians and armed insurgents at the hands of the military, the Brotherhood was defeated.

Between February 1982 and March 2011, the Syrian Brotherhood was an organization in exile, operating outside Syrian borders, and it experienced even more internal divisions.[76] However, when the Arab Spring reached Syria in March of 2011, triggering the Syrian conflict that continues to rage on, the Brotherhood initially only had an external presence. As with the Egyptian Brotherhood in Cairo, the Syrian Brothers were at first reluctant to join an uprising whose success was far from certain. However, that soon changed several months after the beginning of protests across Syria when the Brotherhood helped to co-found the Syrian National Council (SNC) in Istanbul. The SNC became the main opposition coalition that eventually claimed itself to be the legitimate Syrian government in exile. Today, it remains one of the most influential opposition bodies fighting the Assad regime, and it is also suspected to be funding and coordinating with dozens of armed rebel groups on the ground. On March 25, 2012, it issued the "Covenant and Pact," which listed demands, concepts, and goals for a post-Assad Syria; the document called for a "modern, democratic, and pluralistic civil state," and has been described as "the basis for a new social contract, laying the foundations for a modern and secure national relationship between the components of Syrian society."[77]

Thus, despite its turbulent past, as with the Egyptian branch, the Syrian Brotherhood remained resilient, ultimately climbing to a position of power and significant influence within the Syrian opposition. The group has officially formed a political party – the National Party for Justice and the Constitution, or Waad – in preparation for what it hopes will be a transition from the iron grips of Assad. Describing itself as a "national party with an Islamic framework…that adopts democratic mechanisms in its programs," it appears that the group is taking full advantage of the

---

[74] Khaled Yacoub Oweis, "Syria's Muslim Brotherhood Rise from the Ashes," *Reuters*, May 6, 2012, http://www.reuters.com/article/2012/05/06/us-syria-brotherhood-idUSBRE84504R20120506.
[75] Robin Wright, *Dreams and Shadows: The Future of the Middle East* (London: Penguin Press, 2008), 241-248.
[76] Rassas, "Syria's Muslim Brotherhood: Past and Present."
[77] "The Muslim Brotherhood in Syria," *Carnegie Endowment*, accessed September 10, 2014, http://carnegieendowment.org/syriaincrisis/?fa=48370.

spotlight it is under and asserting its democratic agenda, likely to win the support of Western powers and the larger international community.[78] The crucial role of the Syrian Brotherhood in the Syrian conflict, the Brotherhood's role in an eventual post-Assad transition, and the impact a Syrian Brotherhood victory will have on other branches around the world will all be something both Islamists and non-Islamists alike will be looking out for.

The Brotherhood in the Gulf

In Bahrain, the Muslim Brotherhood is represented by al-Eslah Society, which was established in May of 1941 as the first organization in the Gulf affiliated to the Muslim Brotherhood. The society was reportedly founded by Sheikh Abdulrahman al-Jowder, an al-Eslah member who had studied in Cairo, where he met Hassan al-Banna and other Brotherhood leadership. After studying with al-Banna, al-Jowder became inspired to start a branch of his own, and he returned to Bahrain to do just that.[79]

In 2000, the Bahraini royal family formed a council and tasked it with the drafting of a new national charter in line with the government's Reform Project. As other groups and movements began exploring entry into the political arena, the Brotherhood decided to follow suit, and a political wing was established under the name al-Menbar Islamic Society, which the Brotherhood described as "a Bahraini political society representing Islam in the Kingdom of Bahrain built upon the clarity of our vision and our goals, the values derived from Islamic teachings, our political and academic leaders, and our long history in service to the nation and its citizens, seeking to lift the nation, its progress, security and stability."[80] In the 2002 parliamentary elections, al-Menbar was able to win seven seats, and another seven seats in 2006. Though it is not a major political force, al-Menbar and the Bahraini Brotherhood do have some degree of influence in Bahraini politics and society.

What makes Bahrain different from Egypt or Syria, where the Brotherhood has historically been oppressed and banned? In Bahrain, the ruling family has essentially co-opted the Bahraini Brotherhood to maintain a mutually beneficial relationship between the regime and the Brotherhood. The Bahraini branch was one of few political organizations in Bahrain that was permitted to operate for several decades, as political parties were outlawed in Bahrain until the first parliamentary elections in 2002. In fact, some analysts believe that Bahrain's Royal Court and Islamic banking sector are even bankrolling, or at least partially funding, the group.

This government support for the Bahraini Brotherhood reflects the political environment in Bahrain. The country is ruled by the Sunni royal family, but Bahrain is a majority Shiite country, and as such, the Shiites are well represented in parliament. The Brotherhood's al-Menbar Islamic

---

[78] Yezid Sayigh and Raphael Lefevre, "Uncertain Future for the Syrian Muslim Brotherhood's Political Party," *Carnegie Middle East Center*, December 9, 2013, http://carnegie-mec.org/publications/?fa=53850.
[79] "The Brotherhood in Bahrain," *Asharq Al-Awsat*, June 22, 2013, http://www.aawsat.net/2013/06/article55306719.
[80] Ibid.

Society has won seats since its first participation into politics in the 2002 parliamentary elections, and despite its Islamist platform and agenda, the government has supported it, as the al-Menbar has ensured that it takes a supportive position to the monarchy's agenda. Generally, al-Menbar would lend support to the government's various political and economic policies while pursuing its own Islamist social objectives. Therefore, it has become a key pro-regime presence in parliament, and thus, the government has chosen to overlook its Islamist tendencies.[81] Adding to this is the fact that Bahrain, as with the other Gulf countries, is a monarchy, and power and information are both tightly controlled. The environment in Bahrain does not give the local Brotherhood any leeway or options but to cooperate with the government if it wants to keep on operating as a legal political entity. In this way, the circumstances of the Bahraini Brotherhood is similar to those of the Jordanian one, which has also been co-opted by the Jordanian monarchy.

Similarly, in Qatar, the local Brotherhood branch was co-opted by the Qatari regime. However, the Qatari Brotherhood dissolved itself in the early 2000s to avoid a breakdown of relations with the Qatari ruling family at a time when other governments in the region were cracking down on the Brotherhood. Today, Qatari Brotherhood members have found no reason to reform a local chapter again, as they reportedly see "little reason for anti-government agitation in a country that has become host and home to some of the region's most famous Brotherhood figures, that has provided public platforms to these individuals, and whose foreign policy since 2011 has been anchored in support for Islamist groups."[82] Yusuf al-Qardawi, the exiled Egyptian Brotherhood member, is an apt example of the leniency and support Qatar has for the Muslim Brotherhood.

---

[81] Lori Plotkin Boghardt, "The Muslim Brotherhood in the Gulf: Prospects for Agitation," *The Washington Institute*, June 10, 2013, http://www.washingtoninstitute.org/policy-analysis/view/the-muslim-brotherhood-in-the-gulf-prospects-for-agitation.
[82] Ibid.

Yusuf al-Qardawi

In neighboring Kuwait, the Brotherhood has formed a significant presence as well. According to the Washington Institute, "The Kuwaiti Muslim Brotherhood is a superbly organized and extraordinarily wealthy monolith." However, the Kuwaiti branch has perhaps been less cooperative than its counterparts in Bahrain and Qatar, as it has worked with and against the ruling family at various points throughout its history.

That said, the position of the Brotherhood increased remarkably in the 1990s. Following the 1990 invasion of Kuwait by Iraq, the Brotherhood was one of the most active organizations in Kuwait that organized resistance activities against Saddam Hussein's forces and led community services. The Kuwaiti Brotherhood's position was further bolstered by the fact that the two major Brotherhood branches at that time – the Egyptian Brotherhood and the Syrian Brotherhood -- were unable to provide an adequate response to the Iraqi invasion, leaving the matter up to the Kuwaiti branch to resolve on its own. As the former General Guide of the Syrian branch, Ali Saddredine al-Bayanouni, admitted in retrospect, "The first statement we issued, we condemned the occupation of Kuwait by Iraq. We condemned the occupation in a way that might be considered to have been mild."[83] Thus, the Egyptian and Syrian Brotherhoods' lukewarm

---

[83] Pargeter, *The Muslim Brotherhood*, 93.

response to the invasion spurred the Kuwaiti branch to take action, boosting it to a significantly influential position within its country and the region.

Furthermore, at the end of 2012, the Kuwaiti Brotherhood's political wing – the Islamic Constitutional Movement, or Hadas – joined other opposition groups in protesting against the government's ruling on electoral procedures, proving its willingness and ability to network with other opposition factions to achieve a common goal.[84] The Kuwaiti Brotherhood therefore has remained a key player in its country, though it certainly was not immune to the regional backlash against Islamist movements after the fall of the Egyptian Muslim Brotherhood in July 2013. While it is unlikely to be subject to full repression, the Kuwaiti Brotherhood – and other Brotherhood branches in the Gulf – is likely feeling an unfamiliar pressure.

The Gulf has historically been a friendly region for the Brotherhood. Yusuf al-Qardawi, the exiled Egyptian Brotherhood member, and many other exiled Islamists have taken up residence in Qatar and Kuwait. Additionally, since the designation of the Egyptian Muslim Brotherhood as a terrorist organization in December 2013, and Saudi Arabia's own terror designation of the Muslim Brotherhood in 2014, there has been increased pressure on Qatar, Kuwait, and Bahrain to relinquish their support of the Brotherhood. Additionally, in the near future, the security challenge that these Gulf countries face vis-à-vis their respective Brotherhood branches will likely intensify, as the Egyptian Muslim Brotherhood continues to be completely repressed in Egypt.

The Brotherhood in Europe

Since its founding in 1928, the Muslim Brotherhood has profoundly influenced and shaped the beliefs of generations of Islamists across the Middle East. However, in recent decades, it has lost some of its appeal in the region, particularly as it experienced crushing repression from local regimes. Younger generation of Islamists, seeking more action-oriented and radical organizations, thus began to bypass the Brotherhood to explore opportunities with more action-oriented extremist groups like al-Qaeda.

Of course, the Middle East is only one part of the Muslim world, with the other significant parts being South Asia, Europe, and North America. In particular, Europe has become an incubator for Islamist thought, and thousands of Islamists have immigrated to Europe in the past several decades, taking advantage of the liberal environment of the European countries to gather together and refine their Islamist leanings. Since the early 1960s, Muslim Brotherhood members, supporters, and exiles have moved to Europe and slowly but steadily established a well-organized network of mosques, charitable associations, and Islamic organizations. According to Lorenzo Vidino of the Middle East Quarterly: "Four decades of teaching and cultivation have paid off. The student refugees who migrated from the Middle East forty years ago and their

---

[84] Boghardt, "The Muslim Brotherhood in the Gulf: Prospects for Agitation."

descendants now lead organizations that represent the local Muslim communities in their engagement with Europe's political elite. Funded by generous contributors from the Persian Gulf, they preside over a centralized network that spans nearly every European country."[85]

In Germany, in France, and in the U.K., these small branches of the Muslim Brotherhood have established roots and gained acceptance among European governments and media as moderate, religious, and social organizations, despite the fact that much of their manifesto is based off that of the original Egyptian Muslim Brotherhood. As Vidino pointed out, "While they [Muslim Brotherhood members] publicly condemn the murder of commuters in Madrid and school children in Russia, they continue to raise money for Hamas and other terrorist organizations. Europeans, eager to create a dialogue with their increasingly disaffected Muslim minority, overlook this duplicity."[86]

Particularly in Germany, the Muslim Brotherhood has dug its roots deep. More than anywhere else in Europe, the Brotherhood's German branch has gained significant influence, and perhaps more importantly, political acceptance by the people and the media. During the 1950s and 1960s, when Nasser banned the Muslim Brotherhood and the tide turned significantly against the Brotherhood all across the region, thousands of students left the Middle East to flee to Germany. Even after the end of Nasser's era and the rise of the more lenient Sadat, a good majority of Brotherhood members decided to stay in Germany to study in its universities and have a family, particularly because universities in Germany had stellar reputations, but also because Germany since World War II has striven to espouse racial and ethnic equality, making it a comfortable environment for immigrants to live in.

When Germany was still divided into East and West Germany, West Germany in particular welcomed these young Muslims, many of whom were Islamists escaping arrest or assassination of desiring an escape from their repressive regimes. One such Islamist was Sa'id Ramadan, who had served as the personal secretary to Hassan al-Banna, and who had left the Brotherhood in 1948 and moved to Germany to attend law school in Cologne. In Germany, Ramadan went on to found several Muslim organizations and establish a network in Germany and across Europe.[87] In addition to Ramadan, a number of other prominent members of the Syrian Brotherhood also fled to Germany, participating in the Islamist organizations there.

By the 1980s, in Germany and elsewhere in Europe, immigrants who had taken the Muslim Brotherhood to Europe realized that they may never return to their countries of origin. Thus, they began establishing more permanent organizations inspired by the Brotherhood, resulting in the establishment of some of the largest Muslim organizations on the continent, including the Union des Organisations Islamiques de France (Union of French Islamic Organizations, established in

---

[85] Lorenzo Vidino, "The Muslim Brotherhood's Conquest of Europe," *The Middle East Quarterly*, Winter 2005, http://www.meforum.org/687/the-muslim-brotherhoods-conquest-of-europe.
[86] Ibid.
[87] Ibid.

1983), the Islamische Gemeinschaft in Deutschland (Islamic Community in Germany, established in 1982), the Muslim Association of Britain (established in 1997) and the Ligue Islamique Interculturelle de Belgique (Intercultural Islamic League of Belgium, established in 1997).[88]

Although they were started by Brotherhood members, most of these entities are considered loose affiliates rather than formal branches of the Muslim Brotherhood. Their manifestos have become moderate, and the focus has been more on political activism and social services rather than fighting for an upheaval of the current order or actually attempting to establish an Islamic state in their respective countries. The organizations instead act as representative bodies for Muslim populations in each country, and thus focus on advocating for Muslim causes, most of them socially oriented. They engage in a wide range of activities that are designed to serve the daily religious needs of ordinary Muslims, such as operating mosques and prayer halls, organizing and funding afterschool Qur'an and Arabic classes, providing burial services, and so on.[89]

Today, the large Muslim Brotherhood-affiliated organizations in Europe fall under the loose jurisdiction of the Federation of Islamic Organizations in Europe, an umbrella group based in Brussels. Founded in 1989, the Federation represents Muslim organizations in more than two dozen European countries. Though it has suffered from leadership disputes, internal conflicts, and rivalries between its national bodies at various points throughout its history, all of the Federation's constituent organizations have common goals: "promoting Islam as a comprehensive way of life, strengthening the Muslim community in Europe and encouraging Muslims to participate in European society in order to promote Islamic causes."[90]

Other European organizations inspired by the Muslim Brotherhood have established Islamic centers and mosques across the continent to help meet the religious needs of their respective Muslim communities, including organizing religious classes, providing space for libraries supplied with Islamic books, and running shops selling religious items. In addition, as of 2008, it is estimated that about 400 mosques and prayer spaces in Europe were at least indirectly associated with the Muslim Brotherhood, whether in coordinating their creation or funding them.[91] The Brotherhood branches in Europe therefore are more like social movements and less like political parties.

Clearly, the environment in Europe plays a large part in shaping the characteristics of the European Brotherhoods; there is freedom of speech, freedom to organize, and freedom of press

---

[88] Ibid.
[89] "Muslim Brotherhood and Jama'at-i Islami," *Pew Research*, September 15, 2010, http://www.pewforum.org/2010/09/15/muslim-networks-and-movements-in-western-europe-muslim-brotherhood-and-jamaat-i-islami/#expansion-in-europe.
[90] Ibid.
[91] Ibid.

in Europe, so the Brotherhood branches are completely free to gather and voice their thoughts and opinions. However, overthrowing the governments of European countries and establishing Islamic states in their stead is too unrealistic of a goal in a continent where governance is well established. Thus, the Brotherhood branches in Europe have turned their attention from the government and politics to the people and Muslim communities.

Chapter 8: The Future of the Muslim Brotherhood

Despite its turbulent history, the Muslim Brotherhood remains the world's oldest, largest, and best organized transnational Islamist movement. Though founded decades ago by a now deceased Islamic scholar, the group continues to profess its original Islamist slogan: "Allah is our objective, the Koran is our constitution, the Prophet is our leader, struggle [*jihad*] is our way and death for the sake of Allah is the highest of our aspirations."[92]

The future of the Brotherhood would become much clearer if the group were to finally settle itself on a single platform. As a result of being forced to operate underground for decades, the group has suffered from contradictions and controversies throughout much of its history – from changing ideologies to uncertain leadership – so it has long struggled to articulate a single and united stance on many key issues pertaining to Egyptian society, including women's rights and participation in government, the role of non-Muslim and non-Arab minorities, and the nature of a truly Islamic state. It is very much easy to understand then why both Egyptian and international observers have found it difficult to develop a coherent and well-supported stance toward the movement, making it difficult for the Brotherhood to establish ties and expand its support base.

This is another reason why the Brotherhood's future is so tenuous. Due to its fickle views and past contradictory stances, major powers in the West have found it immensely challenging to figure out a response to the oppression of the Brotherhood in Egypt and elsewhere. The crackdown on thousands of alleged Brotherhood members after the fall of Mohamed Morsi has been violent and, more importantly, without firm evidence of crime. Thousands of alleged Brotherhood "supporters" are being arrested and sentenced in speedy trials, without adequate proof that they have been involved in terror activities or that they are even affiliated with the Brotherhood. Had another social or political movement been so severely repressed, Western countries and international organizations would likely develop a fixed policy demanding reform from the Sisi regime, but in Egypt's case, despite hundreds being sent to jail for membership in the Brotherhood and some even sentenced to death, Western nations continue to act with indifference. If the Brotherhood established its platform more clearly, other countries might finally decide whether to oppose or support the organization.

With the Brotherhood's rapid ascent after the Arab Spring came unprecedented challenges that

---

[92] Michael Ryan, "The Muslim Brotherhood and Transition in Egypt," *Middle East Institute*, February 8, 2011, http://www.mei.edu/content/muslim-brotherhood-and-transition-egypt.

it was ultimately unable to overcome. For decades, the group placed great focus on identity and religious politics, stressing Egyptians' Islamic roots, criticizing Western secular values, and calling for an Egypt based solely on legislation compatible with *shari'a*. This broad and unsharpened rhetoric was pushed aggressively, but the group spent little time or effort on developing alternative or realistic policies that were compatible with their views yet feasible in the current geopolitical climate of the 21st century. The Brotherhood's coming to power created new realities for the organization to face, particularly when determining the relationship between religion and state. With its leaders now imprisoned, exiled, or in hiding, and extremist members turning to violence to retake what was lost, the future of the Brotherhood seems bleak. Of course, with that said, the Brotherhood has endured challenges in the past.

The outcome of Egypt's experience in dealing with the Islamists will undoubtedly have regional consequences. Al-Qaeda has already released statements criticizing the crackdown on the Brotherhood and citing the Brotherhood's fall as validation of its own rhetoric that democracy is neither peaceful nor a viable path to power. How the Sisi government turns its overly repressive and anti-Islamist policies into a more inclusive stance will have a great impact on the future of the Brotherhood moving forward.

Bibliography

"Anwar Sadat Killed." *UPI*. 1981. http://www.upi.com/Archives/Audio/Events-of-1981/Anwar-Sadat-Killed.

Beaumont, Peter and Jack Shenker. "Egypt Braces Itself for Biggest Day of Protests Yet." *The Guardian*. January 27, 2011. http://www.theguardian.com/world/2011/jan/27/egypt-protests-biggest-day-yet.

Blair, Edmund. "Tables Turn as Egypt's Islamist President Sworn In." *Reuters*. June 30, 2012. http://www.reuters.com/article/2012/06/30/us-egypt-politics-idUSBRE85S0JP20120630.

Boghardt, Lori Plotkin. "The Muslim Brotherhood in the Gulf: Prospects for Agitation." *The Washington Institute*. June 10, 2013. http://www.washingtoninstitute.org/policy-analysis/view/the-muslim-brotherhood-in-the-gulf-prospects-for-agitation.

De Kerckhove, Ferry. *Egypt's Muslim Brotherhood and the Arab Spring*. Calgary: CDFAI, 2012.

Diagle, Craig. *The Limits of Detente: The United States, the Soviet Union, and the Arab–Israeli Conflict, 1969–1973*. New Haven: Yale University Press, 2012.

"Egypt: Muslim Brotherhood Plans Political Party." *USA Today*. February 15, 2011. http://usatoday30.usatoday.com/news/world/2011-02-15-egypt-muslim-brotherhood_N.htm.

"Egypt Government Declares Muslim Brotherhood 'Terrorist Group.'" *Ahram Online*. December 26, 2013. http://english.ahram.org.eg/News/90037.aspx.

Eikmeier, Dale C. "Qutbism: An Ideology of Islamic-Fascism." *Parameters* (Spring 2007): 85-98.

El Houdaiby, Ibrahim. *From Prison to Palace: The Muslim Brotherhood's Challenges and Responses in Post-Revolution Egypt*. Fride and Hivos, 2013.

El Rashidi, Yasmine. "Egypt: The Rule of the Brotherhood." *The New York Review of Books*. February 7, 2013. http://www.nybooks.com/articles/archives/2013/feb/07/egypt-rule-brotherhood/?pagination=false.

Gordon, Joel. "The False Hopes of 1950: The Wafd's Last Hurrah and the Demise of Egypt's Old Order." *International Journal of Middle East Studies* 21 (1989): 193-214.

"Hassan Al-Banna and His Political Thought of Islamic Brotherhood." *Ikhwan Web*. May 13, 2008. http://www.ikhwanweb.com/article.php?id=17065.

"Hosni Mubarak Resigns as President." *Al-Jazeera*. February 11, 2011. http://www.aljazeera.com/news/middleeast/2011/02/201121125158705862.html.

Ibrahim, Saad Eddin. *Egypt, Islam, and Democracy: Twelve Critical Essays*. Cairo: American University of Cairo Press, 1996.

"Ikhwan Web." Accessed September 6, 2014. http://www.ikhwanweb.com/.

International Crisis Group (ICG). 20 April 2004. "Islamism in North Africa II: Egypt's Opportunity". Cairo/Brussels: International Crisis Group.

International Republican Institute. December 2005. "2005 Parliamentary Election Assessment in Egypt." International Republican Institute Report.

Jansen, Johannes J.G. "The Muslim Brotherhood Movement: A Glance at its History and Ideology." *Gates of Vienna*. http://gatesofvienna.blogspot.jp/2012/07/the-history-and-ideology-of-muslim.html.

Kumar, Medhini, "Evaluating The Muslim Brotherhood's Compatibility With Democracy: An Examination of the Ideologies of Hasan Al-Banna, Seyyid Qutb, and Essam El-Erian." BA diss., Emory College, 2012.

Laub, Zachary. "Egypt's Muslim Brotherhood." *Council on Foreign Relations*. January

15, 2014. http://www.cfr.org/egypt/egypts-muslim-brotherhood/p23991.

Leiken, Robert S. and Steven Brooke. "The Moderate Muslim Brotherhood." *Foreign Affairs.* 2007. http://www.foreignaffairs.com/articles/62453/robert-s-leiken-and-steven-brooke/the-moderate-muslim-brotherhood.

McGreal, Chris and Jack Shenker. "Hosni Mubarak Resigns – and Egypt Celebrates a New Dawn." *The Guardian.* February 11, 2011. http://www.theguardian.com/world/2011/feb/11/hosni-mubarak-resigns-egypt-cairo.

Mitchell, Richard Paul. *The Society of the Muslim Brothers.* New York: Oxford University Press, 1993.

Mura, Andrea. "A Genealogical Inquiry into Early Islamism: The Discourse of Hasan Al-Banna." *Journal of Political Ideologies* 17, no. 1 (20120): 61-85.

"Muslim Brotherhood and Jama'at-i Islami." *Pew Research.* September 15, 2010. http://www.pewforum.org/2010/09/15/muslim-networks-and-movements-in-western-europe-muslim-brotherhood-and-jamaat-i-islami/#expansion-in-europe.

"Muslim Brotherhood's Rashad al-Bayoumi: 'The Revolution Will Continue Until Our Demands Are Met.'" *Spiegel Online International.* February 7, 2011. http://www.spiegel.de/international/world/muslim-brotherhood-s-rashad-al-bayoumi-the-revolution-will-continue-until-our-demands-are-met-a-743919.html.

Norton, Augustus R. *Thwarted Politics: The Case of Hizb al-Wasat. Remaking Muslim Politics: Pluralism, Contestation, Democratization,* R.W. Hefner. Ed. Princeton: Princeton University Press, 2005.

Oweis, Khaled Yacoub. "Syria's Muslim Brotherhood Rise from the Ashes." *Reuters.* May 6, 2012. http://www.reuters.com/article/2012/05/06/us-syria-brotherhood-idUSBRE84504R20120506.

Pargeter, Alison. *The Muslim Brotherhood: From Opposition to Power.* London: Saqi Books, 2013.

Perry, Tom. "Brotherhood Says No Plans for Egypt Presidential Bid." *Reuters.* February 4, 2011. http://af.reuters.com/article/egyptNews/idAFLDE71309L20110204.

Phelan, Shane "'Fatwa' Sheikh with Links to Irish Muslims Is Refused Visa." *Independent.ie.* August 8, 2011. http://www.independent.ie/irish-news/fatwa-sheikh-with-links-to-irish-muslims-is-refused-visa-26759225.html.

"Politics and the Brotherhood in the Mubarak Era." *Islamopedia.* http://www.islamopediaonline.org/country-profile/egypt/politics-and-muslim-brotherhood/politics-and-brotherhood-mubarak-era.

Qutb, Sayyid. "Milestones," in *Political Dissent: A Global Reader: Modern Sources.* Ed. Derek Malone-France. Plymouth: Lexington Books, 2012.

Rassas, Mohammad Saied. "Syria's Muslim Brotherhood: Past and Present." *Al-Monitor.* January 5, 2014. http://www.al-monitor.com/pulse/politics/2014/01/syria-muslim-brotherhood-past-present.html#.

Robbins, James S. "Al-Qaeda Versus Democracy." *The Journal of International Security Affairs* 9 (2005): 53-59.

Ryan, Michael. "The Muslim Brotherhood and Transition in Egypt." *Middle East Institute.* February 8, 2011. http://www.mei.edu/content/muslim-brotherhood-and-transition-egypt.

Sayigh, Yezid and Raphael Lefevre. "Uncertain Future for the Syrian Muslim Brotherhood's Political Party." *Carnegie Middle East Center.* December 9, 2013. http://carnegie-mec.org/publications/?fa=53850.

Shahzad, Syed Saleem. "Jordan's Islamic Front Rallies Muslims." *Asia Times.* March 7, 2003. http://www.atimes.com/atimes/Middle_East/EC07Ak01.html.

Spencer, Richard. "Tunisia Riots: Reform or Be Overthrown, US Tells Arab States Amid Fresh Riots." *The Telegraph.* January 13, 2011. http://www.telegraph.co.uk/news/worldnews/africaandindianocean/tunisia/8258077/Tunisia-riots-Reform-or-be-overthrown-US-tells-Arab-states-amid-fresh-riots.html.

"The Brotherhood in Bahrain." *Asharq Al-Awsat.* June 22, 2013. http://www.aawsat.net/2013/06/article55306719.

"The Camp David Accords of 1979." *BBC News.* November 29, 2001. http://news.bbc.co.uk/2/hi/in_depth/middle_east/israel_and_the_palestinians/key_documents/1632849.stm.

"The Muslim Brotherhood in Syria." *Carnegie Endowment.* Accessed September 10, 2014. http://carnegieendowment.org/syriaincrisis/?fa=48370.

Utvik, Bjorn Olav. "Filling the Vacant Throne of Nasser: The Economic Discourse of Egypt's Islamist Opposition." *Arab Studies Quarterly* 17, no. 4 (Fall 1995): 25-94.

Vidino, Lorenzo. "The Muslim Brotherhood's Conquest of Europe." *The Middle East Quarterly.* Winter 2005. http://www.meforum.org/687/the-muslim-brotherhoods-conquest-of-europe.

Wedeman, Ben, Reza Sayah, and Matt Smith. "Coup Topples Egypt's Morsy; Deposed President under 'House Arrest.'" *CNN.* July 4, 2013. http://edition.cnn.com/2013/07/03/world/meast/egypt-protests/index.html?hpt=hp_t1.

Williams, Helen. "Egypt's Unprecedented Execution Verdicts." *Al-Monitor.* March 24, 2014. http://www.al-monitor.com/pulse/originals/2014/03/egypt-executions.html#.

Worth, Robert F. "How a Single Match Can Ignite a Revolution." *The New York Times.* January 21, 2011. http://www.nytimes.com/2011/01/23/weekinreview/23worth.html?src=twrhp&_r=0.

Wright, Robin. *Dreams and Shadows: The Future of the Middle East.* London: Penguin Press, 2008.

CPSIA information can be obtained at www.ICGtesting.com
Printed in the USA
LVOW07s1544280715

447956LV00017B/1071/P